AMERICA IS CRAZY COOL!

by Mysterious Q

About Me

I call myself Q because I am a Star Trek Fan. No, I'm not a Trekker or Trekkie, just a fan. I don't have a copy of Spock Sings!, but enjoy the "Q" Character from Star Trek: The Next Generation. I like the way he is all powerful, all-knowing, sarcastic and always trying to help humans improve themselves in his own way. Kinda like me! Well, maybe alittle. My real name is not important. Call me Q because it makes me feel self-important and omnipotent (like most Politicians). I am at times serious, sarcastic or just full of myself. That is the way I survive mentally in a world where U.S. Presidents get extra-marital blow jobs in the Blue Room and Billion Dollar Companies get bail-outs.

I'm not about being a republican, democrat, independent or whatever. I'm about being American and being fed up with loser Politicians whose only goals are self-enrichment and the promotion of their personal political views. They have forgotten what it means to be an American and I am here to try and remind them. Or, maybe I'm just here to remind you what America could be if we all tried harder and elected people that actually cared. Being elected doesn't mean you get to stop listening to the people that put you there and do what you want or what your party wants you to do. O.K. Enough for now.

Introduction

I believe in America. America has made my fortune. And I raised my daughter in the American fashion...Oops...Sorry, that was from The Godfather. Crazy is as crazy does. Let me start again. I LOVE AMERICA! It just rocks, but stupid jerk-bag politicians and other idiots are trying to destroy it! Instead of helping them by voting for the next fat cat that runs for offer, I have decided to go on the attack...

I am not a marital artist, if I tried to be they would call be Bruce IcouldNotBe (Lee). Sorry again, I am just hitting a wall here trying to figure out how to sound cool and hip in my introduction. Guess that's a no go. Well, anyway, I have one talent and it is writing. I am NOT a good writer, just an impassioned one and sometimes that enough.

Let me inspire you to stop electing idiots and start fighting the power with your words and deeds. Inspire others to vote for the little guys that represent the real America, not the one occupied by Gzillianaires who have never had to worry about their bills or what their family will eat because mommy or daddy is paying the bills. Go to rallies and question the people who the powers that be put up for election: Ask them how they can relate to you and other average Americans?

Now look, I am not some kind of half-baked socialist or right wing Kool Aid drinker...actually...I don't know what I am? But I do know that I love America and that it is the coolest place ever to live. If you feel the same, you will probably love this book and get inspired by it. If you don't, go hug a tree, hit a pillow or join a neighborhood watch and shoot somebody. Meanwhile, visit my web site at http://gthomy.tripod.com/pp/pp.html and there will be no nuclear war...ever!

Chapter One: The Blind Leading The Blind

When it rains, it pours and it now appears that our dysfunctional government is even more messed up than anyone could have imagined. While campaign ads run ahead of this year's big election touting the wondrous accomplishments of the powers that be, us regular folk are left to ponder the million dollar parties held by the GSA while half of all American families are living at the poverty level or below and the paid female entertainment specialists engaged by the Secret Service are getting STIFFED for their fees (can a video or calendar of those hot girls be far off?). But now, there's more...

Just when you thought it was safe to watch the news there are more government debacles to consider of equal or greater stupidity. This time the GSA big spenders are back for another round of dumbness with kickbacks, while the geniuses that dictate our foreign policy are screwing up everything everywhere and the FAA got caught with its Fly open proving they are just for the birds.

Now I know where those gavones at the GSA got all that extra cash to party hardy... The Washington Business Journal reports that the GSA was getting around nineteen percent in kickbacks from contractors that were permitted to claim a special energy-efficient tax deduction. They had to write a check to the GSA for the cash value of the deduction. Wow, and I thought that only the Mafia knew how to put the squeeze on legitimate contractors. Still, I guess I would rather have my contract canceled by the GSA than the Godfather.

If you are going to make a mess of something, I say go all the way! It looks like All The President's Men (oops, forgot Ms. Clinton) are taking that advice big time. There's a little trouble in Big Red China. The blind Chinese dissident who decided to escape and hold up at the U.S. Embassy in the land of the pagoda just before this year's big meet and greet between Beijing and Washington has everyone all atwitter.

First they say Chen Guangcheng asked for Political Asylum, then they say he left the building (the embassy folks probably out too much MSG in their food) saying he was told by someone at the State Department that the Chinese Government was threatening to kill his family. So says the news media, but who knows? Nobody can get a straight answer out of any of the parties involved in this situation. The good news is that the Chinese Foreign Ministry now says the dissident can apply to come to the USA as a student. It's unclear whether or not his family will be able to join him or if he will actually be able to leave.

My wife met some Chinese students from Red China (yes folks, it's still a Communist Nation) when she was still in college in Arizona. They were brought to school each day on a bus, followed around by Chinese security, not given a chance to casually interact with us scheming capitalists and watched closely until the bus came to pick them up at the end of classes. I guess they did all that in case those young people were homesick and wanted a taste of Marxism here in the land of the free and home of the naive.

While all this stuff is going on in Beijing, the Russians decide to get feisty and show the world that they know how to make headlines as good or better than everybody else. Russian senior military commander General Nikola Makarov warned that if the the USA sets up a planned missile defense system in Europe, he will launch a first strike to take it out. He went on to say that any NATO bases hosting that system would be legitimate first strike targets. Whatever happened to Perestroika? And everyone thought that Bush II was the only one ruining America's image abroad. Maybe so, but he didn't have the Russians ready to launch missiles at us!

Not only have our fearless leaders been spreadin' the love abroad, but they are making friends and influencing idiocy here at home as well. A passenger who filmed a recent bird strike on an airliner this past April and released it to the media received a nasty letter from the FAA. Grant Cardone was probably expecting a thank you note for filming something which could potentially be used to examine exactly how bird strikes impact airliners, but instead he received a reprimand for not properly stowing away his iPad before the plane took off. Given that most airline passengers are treated like meat in a seat on flights these days, that doesn't surprise me.

It's no wonder that a recent TV series called Pam Am failed to attract enough of an audience to avoid cancellation. Anyone who watched it probably thought the network and the series was making all that stuff up about how Stewardesses and Stewards (OMG...I mean Flight Attendants...sorry!) once treated their customers. Today's flight crews are more like the matron you would find at theaters years ago. During Matinee showings they would go around pointing a flashlight at kids that talked too much. Anyone that threw popcorn at them would probably get clunked on the head with the same flashlight.

Chapter Two: D.C. Becomes Party Town USA at the Taxpayer's Expense

Every year a survey comes out that recognizes the colleges and universities that are the best and biggest party schools. Not wanting to be left out and perhaps because it is a major source of funding for the students that attend those institutions of getting higher learning and letting the good times roll, it looks like Washington D.C. has thrown their hat into the yearly survey fling ring.

If recent reports about the GSA and Secret Service are true, party schools have a long way to go to catch up with some government bureaucrats. I don't know how much the average college student spends for all the partying they do, but I'm sure it doesn't come close to what a GSA employee spends for the same good time. In fact, if how much you spend on partying counts towards choosing a winner for the biggest party monster, I say that the GSA workers are way ahead of the schools and the Secret Service. According to their own figures, we're talking millions of bucks for galactic class getaways that have been a part of that agency's spending habits for years.

Not to be out done, it looks like some Secret Services agents are trying for first runner up status when it comes to being party animals. They may not spend like the GSA, but they sure know how to have a good time when they travel. In fact, they manage to mix business and pleasure which might actually place them ahead of the GSA party animals when it comes to letting the good times roll.

Anyone that thought the Secret Service were some kind of boring, crewcut, robotic folks that just stood around grimacing and looking tough in off the rack suits while talking into their Dick Tracy style wrist radios hasn't kept up with the times. The new breed of agents dress very dapper, smile occasionally and know how to keep the good times rolling. So say reports that claim the advance team that came to the nation of Colombia to prepare the way for President Obama weren't just busy checking out empty rooms, manhole covers and rooftops, they were also busy mingling with the local population. To be more specific, the working girls!

I have to admit that I have a whole new view of President Obama these days. I figured his first term would be boring and a lot like Bill Clinton's time in the White House, except for the Monica thing and that nasty little impeachment episode. I expected some political drama created by all the wide-eyed socialist wannabees Obama was sure to hire on, but not much more. With the President being a family man, it was unlikely that he would provide us with the kind of personal scandal that Clinton did. However, it now appears that our President is not just the Commander in Chief, but the Master of Ceremonies for one big party!

f the buck stops at the Oval Office like the plaque on President Harry Truman's desk once indicated, I guess that President Obama is a lot less boring and a lot more fun than we all thought possible and I am glad. When Bush (2) was in office the best we could expect from him was that he would say something that sounded really dumb and get a few laughs from that. So when a straight shooter and intelligent man like Obama took office I thought for sure the D.C. good times were over, but was I ever wrong!

If the news reports are true, those party monsters at the GSA spend more time and money having fun than doing anything else. I really wish I had applied for one of those jobs. I mean how much better can it be than getting paid to party and spend lots of money. If the You Tube videos are any indication of how things work at the GSA, it looks to me like the employees that spend the most taxpayer money and have the best times are the ones who get the most kudos. I'll bet that requests for job applications from the GSA are going the roof (if it's still on the building and hasn't been blown off by all the partying).

I don't think it will be the same way at the Secret Service office. It looks like the Prez is a bit miffed at the fact that his advance agents were having too much of a good time with the working girls in Columbia. Although I am sure there will be lots of job openings after that scandal is settled, I doubt that any of the new hires or replacements will have the same perks enjoyed by those guys who ordered the ultimate room service.

When asked to comment on the situation involving the naughty agents, President Obama said he would be angry if it was true that agents brought Prostitutes back to their hotel rooms. I wonder if that is politically-correct speak for "Do what you want on your own time, just don't embarrass me or get caught." Either way, it's too late. The President, the Secret Service and the people of the United States are embarrassed. And it's not even clear if the agents involved were on or off duty when they ordered in. If they were working, I hope they got receipts!

Chapter Three: The Secret Service Agents and The Hot Girls: A Match Made In Heaven

On the heels of the revelations that an advance team of Secret Service Agents and some members of the U.S. Military on duty in Columbia to make the way safe for the President of the United States had contact and at least one dispute with local prostitutes, we are now being told that it may have happened before. The Secret Service says that it is investigating reports that some of their agents may have had contact, and a conflict or two, with some ladies of the night in El Salvador.

Although it is not yet entirely clear whether these people were actually agents or just Secret Service employees, it seems that those nasty boys and some 'military specialists' were partying hard at a strip club somewhere in El Salvador. At some point they decided to visit a private section of the establishment where sexual favors are offered for a price. Maybe they thought that some threat to the President existed there? If it did, they were it! Haven't any of these brain trusts ever seen those old movies where Russian secret agents use prostitutes to get the goods on American diplomats and intelligence operatives?

I think that the real reason the agents go to clubs like the ones in Columbia and El Salvador is because they just don't want to miss out on the party. It has been reported that members of the Drug Enforcement Agency, some U.S. Embassy personnel and other folks from the good old USA visit that naughty den of iniquity all the time. It just makes sense that the Secret Service should be represented there as well.

I am almost certain that this is just the tip of the iceberg. If these shenanigans went on in Columbia and El Salvador, who is to say that they didn't happen just about everywhere else the Secret Service visits to keep the Prez safe. I wonder if there is some Secret Service super secret list of hot places and hot women to visit when you are out and about abroad? If there is, imagine the money that could be made by selling that list.

I think that all the congressional types looking into the Secret Service scandal should order those agents to turn over that list (if it exists) so that the government printing office can make copies and sell it. I am pretty sure that businessmen traveling overseas would pay a fair sum of money for it and that would help reduce the national debt. In fact, I also sure that their wives would pay even more for the list so that they could use it in divorce proceedings.

Now don't get me wrong. I am all for spreading the love and helping foreigners to understand how Americans feel about truth, justice and the American Way, but I am not sure this is the best way to do it. First off, I am a bit concerned about the morality question. I always thought that Secret Service Agents were supposed to be these straight-shooter types that had some kind of written or unwritten code of conduct that made them set a higher standard for behavior than everybody else. You know, like that whole 'officer and a gentleman' thing the military has?

Secondly, I was really upset when the news media reported that one or more Secret Service agents hired a prostitute in El Salvador, had their fun, and then refused to pay her. When she made a fuss, some reports say that they threw her out of a moving car. Now is that any way to treat a lady (even a lady of the evening)? What kind of message does that send to foreign governments? It tells them we are cheap and do not keep our commitments. If some foreign diplomats or secret service agents for some other country hired an escort in some place like New

York or Washington, D.C., refused to pay her and threw her out of a moving car, they would be instantly deported and any future access to Playboy Clubs would be denied worldwide.

Thirdly, I am worried about the costs of all this fun. If the agents are paying for the booze and babes themselves, well, who is to judge how a guy spends his hard-earned money? But if they are somehow charging all this to the taxpayers, I say it's time to cut them off. It's bad enough having to pay taxes to support all those million dollar GSA shindigs while a lot of us can't pay our rent, mortgage or utility bills, but I cannot wrap my mind around the idea of having to pay for the sexual enjoyment of Secret Service Agents and others designated to keep our fearless leader safe.

Finally, I can't understand why these agents, members of the military and other government types feel they have to find their lovin' and pay for it outside the country when we have so many girls that just want to have fun right here. In fact, I have just the thing for lonely Secret Service Agents and other government and military guys who have some extra cash available and are in need of more than just a group hug.

Enter the Hot Girls. In case you haven't seen the 'Hot Problems' music video on YouTube, it's a must-see. The video features a performance by two girls that describe themselves as 'Hot Hot Hot Hot...' and provides those watching it with a short list of problems faced by good looking young women. After the watching the video a few (hundred) times, it seemed to me that these gals need to meet some guys that are also 'Hot Hot Hot Hot...' and, based on all the recent reports about their behavior, who can be considered more desirable and ready to rumble than those wild and crazy Secret Service Agents and other government dudes protecting the president?

Look, we have just got to get these guys and girls together. The most it will probably cost the agents and other government guys is a night or two on the town and that's money well spent for a product made right here in the good old USA. Not only will it keep the Secret Service and military guys from getting in trouble overseas, but it will help save the taxpayers money by eliminating the need for us to pay for their sexcapades and all the congressional inquiries and special investigations that result from them.

It also makes good fiscal sense for the agents, military guys and other government employees to spent their money at home because it helps grow the economy here. As long as taxpayers do have to foot the bill, that is money well spent on the 'Hot Girls' and might help those young women, the agents and military guys all solve some of their "Hot Problems."

Watch the Hot Problems video here: http://gthomy.tripod.com/pp/hotproblems.html

Chapter Four: No Passports, Hugs or Gender Specific Rest Rooms For YOU!

If you owe, you can't go! The IRS has just announced that people who owe them more than fifty thousand dollars will not be issued a passport if they request one. This is just another big government step towards making it a crime to owe the government money, even if you do not really owe them a cent and have been falsely accused of some bogus debt.

The IRS has ruined the lives of many Americans by going after them for tax bills that some have never actually owed. That's why most of these kinds of cases end up in some sort of litigation and appear to go on forever. I think it is completely ridiculous to make people that want or need to travel abroad for their livelihood wait until a debt situation with the IRS is resolved.

What this is really about is the IRS version of a quick fix to filling the national coffers with money gleaned from alleged tax debts that may or may not be owed. Note that they are targeting people with large outstanding tax bills who probably have substantial assets and can afford to pay them right away if they choose that option. It's a case of pay first and dispute the debt later or you get no passport.

Student loan collections will be next. While it's true that there are more than a few people that owe and cannot pay their student loans, it also true that the federal government has helped to create the horrendous economic climate we all must live with. They allowed banks and lenders to go on and on with un-ethical and impractical financial transactions designed to full their own pockets with no regard for the larger economic consequences until the bottom dropped out of our economy.

Those owing money for student loans are already penalized though a process that applies any tax refunds owed to them to their loan debt. Since many of these people are anything but rich, this process basically punishes the poor and rewards the wealthy. Like most big government efforts to exert financial and social control over their citizens, it discriminates against the people that are most vulnerable.

It is not hard to imagine that student loan debtors who owe extremely large sums may ultimately face more sanctions like the denial of professional or even driver license renewals. While complaining about student loan dead beats, the big government supporters fail to recognize their part in that debt. They have helped to create a culture of education that seeks to keep students in school as long as possible whether they have a specific career direction or not.

Big government ideology is like a cancer that is rapidly spreading from the federal level to states and towns which are considering or actually enacting all kinds of new laws and rules to modify our behavior to their liking. A good example is the attack on religion. Big government socialists are trying to create a religiously neutral society where public displays of faith are illegal and religious organizations must conform to whatever politically correct rules and regulations are deemed necessary.

Churches and religious groups are being forced to disregard their own beliefs in favor of 'fairness' as defined by Big Brother. Options for health care procedures like Abortions and the offering of various Birth Control methods that many religious people find repugnant are some of things that big government is trying to force on institutions with religious affiliations. Faith based clubs and groups are being barred from meeting in public facilities or forced by schools to accept members who might be doctrinally opposed to their creed in the name of fairness and equality.

Religion is not the only target of big government socialists. They are absolutely intent on creating a gender neutral society. Many schools around the USA have already tried to create rest rooms for people who cannot make up their mind which gender they wish to associate with. Most have failed, but I am sure they will eventually succeed and those doors will just have the drawing of a toilet on them with a question mark below.

You might think that these ideologues favor one group or another, but for them it is not about being gay, lesbian or straight: It's about being neutral. They believe that the problems which exist by being associated with one sexual preference over another can be solved by creating an asexual society where sexual orientation is limited to the bedroom and no one needs to openly display their choices. That's why many public and even some private schools and facilities are now beginning to try and ban public displays of affection.

An eighth grade student in North Carolina was recently suspended from school for trying to hug his teacher after she broke up a scuffle he was loosing in the hallway. Instead of accepting the hug, she dragged him off to the Principal's Office where the suspension was ordered. Other students around the USA have been reprimanded for hand-holding, pats on the shoulder and even high fives. Hugs and shoulder pats and high fives, oh my! I just glad that none of them were kissing. They probably would have been flogged with a steel whip for that.

Chapter Five: Supreme Stupidity: The U.S. High Court Trashes Your Rights Again

It's no surprise that the Judicial Legislature better known as the U.S. Supreme Court has, yet again, trashed the rights of Americans. It wasn't enough that they managed to give teeth to over-reaching eminent domain laws making privately owned property as non-existent here in the USA as it is in the UK, where the reining Monarch has final authority and ownership over all lands. Now the jerky judges bring you strip searches for everyone.

It doesn't matter if you are justly or unjustly accused of a crime, stopped for a traffic violation, owe a fine or just killed five hundred people in cold blood, you CAN be strip searched by Police for any or no reason at all if they drag you to the station house. That means that whether they search you for legitimate reasons, or just want to COP a feel, you can be strip-searched and probably violated. So make sure you don't give your local police any reason to become annoyed with you. You might want to bath first and put on a fresh set of clothes before going out from now on.

Not only is this Supreme Court ruling beyond stupid in terms of providing police with a tool for instant revenge against anyone that even looks at them the wrong way, it also endangers the very people it is designed to help. The idea behind the ruling is to keep police officers and the environment in which they operate safe from people concealing weapons, drugs or other dangerous contraband. It's also supposed to help protect other detainee's and municipal employees from those same threats, but will strip searches really work?

We have witnessed many high speed chases, shootouts and other dangerous circumstances that occur when a suspect refuses to go quietly for fear of being arrested. Now the supremely stupid blockheads on our high court with low I.Q.s provide yet another reason for people to resist arrest. Fear of the humiliation involved in being strip-searched. While the procedure might cause most of us embarrassment or inconvenience, there are people out there that would rather die (or kill) than submit to a strip-search.

I cannot recall any incident in recent memory where anyone being brought into a police facility or court for a traffic ticket or overdue fine (and not wanted for anything else) has concealed a weapon and shot the place up. I can recall many instances where alleged perpetrators managed to over-power the officer or officers guarding them or gain access to a weapon in the same manner and cause all kinds of mayhem. Perhaps the Supreme Idiots should review the laws on hiring police and court officers to be sure that anyone wanting the job is at least six feet tall, works out ten hours a day and can take on Mike Tyson and win. That would be as unfair to law enforcement officer candidates as their interpretation on strip-searches is to the average citizen.

I was amused recently when the President of the United States complained about the Supreme Court acting as judicial legislators in the matter of his health care bill. He obviously fears that hey will strike down part or all of it. Yet he is not concerned about the decision made by those same judges regarding strip-searches. It's a decision that removes yet another right from Americans in terms of unreasonable searches which had amounted to a safeguard against the abuse of police powers.

The Supreme Court Justices appear to be far more interested in how their judicial colleagues around the world will view their decisions than how those rulings will affect their fellow Americans. It's no secret that many Federal Judges use decisions made by foreign courts and based on the laws of other nations in reaching their own. I guess they think it takes a village to teach a constitutionally-sound judicial decision for Americans (or maybe some village idiots?). I would tell you to vote these knuckle heads out, but you can't. Oh well, democracy was nice while it lasted.

Chapter Six: Are Real 'Hunger Games' In Our Future?

ust in case you do not own a television set, haven't been to the movies since they stopped showing cartoons before the feature presentation or don't read much, "The Hunger Games" has become the Harry Potter franchise of the twenty-first century. The wildly popular book series written for the young adult market by Suzanne Collins spins a post-apocalyptic yarn around sixteen year old Katniss Everdeen.

The stories take place in the nation of Panem where the countries of North America once existed. The Capital is a technologically advanced city that exercises totalitarian control over the twelve impoverished districts surrounding it. Each year one boy and one girl from each of those districts compete in The Hunger Games. The contestants must be twelve to eighteen years of age and are chosen by lottery. The games are a televised outdoor battle to the finish with only one winner.

almost always enjoy post-apocalyptic books and films. It's fascinating to see how they have evolved as different threats, real or imagined, confront humanity. "Planet of the Apes" envisioned a future where humans destroyed the Earth with nukes and another species took over. "Soylent Green" focused on a society brought to the brink of extinction by over-population and pollution. "Mad Max" pointed to the kind of anarchy that might replace law and order in the wake of a societal breakdown. "The Host" tells a tale of Aliens taking over the Earth and seeking human vessels to house their souls.

I think it would be fair to say that George Orwell's book "Nineteen Eighty-Four" should be considered the father of many of these tales and certainly a forerunner of "The Hunger Games." That's because his book also envisions a dark future where large mega-nations replace individual countries and totalitarian regimes control everyone. Although Eric Arthur Blair writing under his "George Orwell" pen name authored the book in 1949, there can be little doubt that he had his finger on the pulse of where humanity was heading. He impressively predicted some political realities we all live with today.

Orwell's nightmarish world of opposites includes an elite ruling class that promises prosperity while destroying the economy and offers freedom through individual, political and social oppression. The Big Brother regime tightly controls its citizens by using various specialized agencies including the Ministry of Truth which oversees propaganda and historical revision (lies), the Ministry of Love which is all about brainwashing and torture (hate), and the Ministry of Peace which conducts foreign policy (war).

The oppressive Orwellian world found in "Nineteen Eighty-Four" also includes things like video screens that simultaneously propagandize and spy on citizens, the Newspeak language that easily foreshadows politically-correct speech, a recognizable form of political-correctness known as Doublethink and the Thought Police who are always ready to pounce on any freethinkers. While it's easy for readers to recognize the many contradictions found in the political system described in "Nineteen Eighty-Four," it is not as easy for the citizens of Oceania to tell the good guys from the bad or the right from the wrong after years of being spoon fed half-truths and outright lies.

I look at "The Hunger Games" as being much more basic and less complicated than "Nineteen Eighty-Four." Considering the dumbing-down of society, that would be a must for any author who wanted to sell books to young people these days. That comment is not a criticism of the book series, just a fair sociological observation. Despite its simplicity and characters that are attractive to a younger audience, "The Hunger Games" offers a warning (whether intentional or not) that is similar to the one found in Orwell's book and often repeated elsewhere: "Power tends to corrupt, and absolute power corrupts absolutely." Those words were first uttered by Sir John Dalberg-Acton, a British historian, politician and writer.

I cannot speak for other nations, but here in America the loss of rights and freedoms is an on-going, candy-coated process that has been fueled by a misguided attempt to eliminate possible threats by limiting individual liberties. As in Orwell's fictional world of opposites, we are informed that in order to properly protect ourselves from evildoers and be good citizens we must allow the government to have more control over our lives. At the same time we are also told that we must give those likely to do us the most harm the benefit of the doubt; that the rights of those who hate and are trying to kill us must be protected while our own liberties are restricted or taken away entirely.

The insane political landscape described in "Nineteen Eighty-Four" is quickly becoming a normal part of everyday life in twenty-first century America. I just wonder how long it will be before the self-serving ideological clones that are running democracy into the ground in the USA and elsewhere find a way to bring some reality-television hell like "The Hunger Games" to life in order to forward their own agendas? I would tell you to use your vote to change things, but I believe that time is past. The powers that be are in complete control and I am sorry to say that they are running the lives of average Americans right into the ground.

Chapter Seven: Drug Tests For Federal Pay Checks

It's election season and once again the USA presidential candidates and politicians running for reelection are bringing out all their most brilliant ideas and policy planks. The most recent suggestion to be added to this brain trust of little wonders is the idea that anyone receiving any sort of federally-funded benefits should be drug tested before they get the government gold. So, I have a question: Are federal paychecks, foreign aid, military aid and humanitarian assistance for other nations included in that list of benefits?

Even if we limit drug testing for federal money to everyone here at home, let's do the right thing. If we are going to give everyone in the USA that receives taxpayer money a drug test, let's be fair and include everyone from the President on down. They receive paychecks drawn on accounts funded with taxpayer money and, as far as I am concerned, what's good for the goose is good for the gander! But let's not stop there...

How about drug tests for all the people, nations and corporations that receive federal money in one form or another? What's wrong with that? If someone receiving unemployment benefits or food stamps takes some cold medicine, fails a drug test and does not get to eat or have a place to live as a result, than I think it is only fair that everyone else that receives money from the government should be punished in the same way if they fail the same test.

Excuse me for asking, but whatever happened to fairness and equality? Those terms used to mean something in the USA. Now they are only used by candidates or politicians when they feel like supporting some plank in their policy agenda designed to appeal to certain groups of voters. Well, I think it's time to take a few of their policy planks and whack the candidates, politicos, pundits and politicians in the head with them. That is the only way that I can think of knocking some sense into these people and getting them to face the same realities that all of the rest of us who don't live in Washington, D.C. Wonderland must face each and every day.

It amazes me that with gasoline costing five dollars per gallon and people having to cut back on everything including essentials like food and housing that the candidates who want our votes have the nerve to start spouting what they know to be outrageous ideas just to get a few votes from one side or the other. Instead of addressing and trying to do something about real life economic issues that mean life or death for many of their fellow Americans, they start talking about drug tests for federal benefits.

Don't get me wrong. I am anti-drug all the way. I do not use alcohol, drugs or believe that the use of weed for medicinal purposes is a good idea. I also think that we are a nation that has become far too dependent on prescription medications. People take pills for anything and everything. Doctors now prescribe so many pills that the world's largest drug companies cannot produce enough for everyone.

All that being said, I do not think it is fair in any way, shape or form to make people who receive federally funded benefits like food stamps to take drug tests unless you are willing to give those same tests to everyone else receiving federal money, including paychecks. I would love to watch the President, Senators, members of Congress and Supreme Court Judges line up to pee and sweat out getting their money the way average Americans might have to if each paycheck required a drug test. And why stop there?

Let's require drug tests for anyone and everyone who receives money from the United States Government, including those who receive foreign aid, military aid and even help in the form of items paid for with government bucks. After all, I do not believe that people waiting to get food stamps or unemployment benefits should be treated any different from people living in other nations who benefit from U.S. aid programs. In fact, I say give all the citizens of every country that receives U.S. aid drug tests and if even one fails, they don't get the money!

If the candidates and politicians are worried about giving federal funds to drug addicts, let's get down to it. Let's begin testing all the people of other nations and employees of all the companies in this world that benefit from the big spenders in Congress and the White House that have billions for them, but can't do anything about the tens of thousands of Americans who have nothing to eat tonight or are living in their cars.

Chapter Eight: The Afghanistan Koran Burnings: Facts verses Fiction

Once again followers of the 'Religion of Peace' are not acting very peaceful. Reacting to what has been characterized as an "accidental" burning of copies of the Koran kept in an Afghan Prison library, 'Islamic Protesters' as they have been described by most of the mainstream

Western News Media have been on the rampage in Afghanistan. At least two Americans have been killed and others injured as Muslims seek revenge for what they believe was a horrendous sacrilege committed by members of the U.S. Forces stationed in that country. Are they justifiably angry?

Let's begin with the actions that lead to the current wave of protests and killings. Were copies of the Koran 'accidentally' burned by U.S. Forces and, if so, was this a sacrilegious act? No and no. According to statements by various military personnel on the ground in Afghanistan the copies of the Koran that were burned had already been desecrated by Muslim Inmates held at an Afghan Prison run by U.S. forces. It is forbidden to write in the pages of the Koran, but that is exactly what these Inmates did.

According to Sky News, a U.S. Official in Afghanistan stated that the Inmates used copies of the Koran and various other religious books and periodicals located in the prison library to pass messages to each other. Not only is this against the prison rules, but writing anything in a copy of the Koran flies directly in the face of Islamic Law. The only proper way to dispose of a Koran that has been desecrated in that manner is for it to be burned, buried or stored. At least that's what many Muslim Clerics claim.

As a result of the Inmate desecration of the copies of the Koran in the prison library, members of the U.S. Military originally said that the decision was made to burn them along with the other books and materials that Inmates incorrectly and illegally used to pass written messages. This was done with the greatest respect and based on research done on the proper way to dispose of a Koran that had been desecrated in that manner. However, now other military spokespeople are saying the whole thing was a mistake.

Even if the military has changed their story, there was still nothing wrong with burning copies of the Koran that had been desecrated by the Afghan Inmates. It was and remains a proper disposal method that is recommended by Muslim Clerics. The other methods of disposal such as indefinite storage or even burial would not have been appropriate due to the sensitive nature of what was written in the copies of the Koran from that prison library. Burning was a fair and reasonable choice given the circumstances. It was not the best choice as far as public relations is concerned, but it is acceptable and certainly not a reason for Muslims to riot and kill.

As a Christian, I believe that my own Holy Book teaches certain things and draws a clear line between right and wrong. I am as committed to the teachings and principles in The Bible as I am sure that Muslims are to the beliefs espoused in the Koran. For example, I believe that the Bible teaches against the practice of drinking alcoholic beverages. What should I do if I walk past a bar with a copy of The Bible in my hand, see people drinking and they happen to make some nasty comment to me about the Word of God? Do I have the right or responsibility to come back later and blow up that bar or murder the patrons inside by shooting them? Of course not.

My Bible teaches that revenge and retribution belongs to God. I do not know enough about the Koran to say what it does or does not teach, but since Muslims believe that their religion is the Religion of Peace I cannot understand how they justify the continued murder of people on God's behalf. Perhaps they believe that peace can only be achieved when everyone is Muslim and all other religions have been eradicated from the face of the Earth. If that is the case, I beg to differ.

I just wonder how long the Political Correctness Police in the main stream Western Media are going to sit back and watch Americans get killed by being bombed, shot or having their heads cut off by believers in the Religion of Peace before that say that kind of behavior is not acceptable for religious or any other reasons. It's bad enough that the people they call 'Islamic Extremists' continually murder each other in the name of their religion, but when they target Americans trying to give them a free and decent place to live, I say it's time to leave them to their own devices.

You can argue about religion and pit one set of beliefs against another until doomsday, but the moment you kill in the name of God you step over the line in a civilized world. If you want to live in a place that is intolerant of other religions, kills someone just for converting to another faith or fails to recognize the same rights for women that they do for men, go ahead and establish some Islamic Republic and leave the rest of us alone. But don't think you can export terrorism in the name of Islam and expect the rest of the world to go along with it.

Chapter Nine: Here's Some Advice For The 2012 and Future Presidential Candidates: Learn A Lesson From George Bailey

It's bad enough that yet another USA Presidential Election season has rolled around to torture us all with all those nasty political ads, but now we have to listen to the stupid comments made by the idiots that are running for office as well. You would think that potential candidates who would do or say anything to get elected would have the good sense to utter words of wisdom instead of the usual verbal blunders, but that's too much to hope for in a nation of people who are more interested in what Lady Gaga will where on her next big TV gig than whether potential presidential candidates can even pass a simple intelligence test.

There are always issues or groups that these politicos love to target and I guess the poor are in their cross hairs this time around. It's sad enough that some idiot recently wrote a book calling people who receive food stamps Moochers, but now good ole Mitt Romney has to chime in by tating, "I'm not concerned about the very poor, we have a safety net there." Oh, really? And where might that be? Maybe I should go and ask the thousands of homeless people currently living precariously on the outskirts of Las Vegas?

Of course we have politicians to thank for allowing and even helping big corporations to trash our economy and cause those millions of fore closures that have created huge homeless enclaves like the one in Vegas. Just to be sure the icing is put on the Las Vegas poverty cake, our beloved fearless leader goes and says, "When times are tough, you tighten your belts...You don't blow a bunch of cash on Vegas when you're trying to save for college."

Oh, thanks for the financial tip Mr. President! Here's one for you: Instead of giving billions of bucks to help bail out huge corporations that have helped to destroy our economy, how about providing some low interest loans so that some of your voters can actually afford to put a roof over their heads and take proper care of their families? You know how them 'Moochers' love free hand-outs! Oh, I forgot. They don't need any freebies because they already have that 'safety net.'"

Perhaps I am a bit jaded, but after watching politicians do their thing for the fifty some years I have existed on this earth I have come to a simple conclusion regarding their moral character: There are few or none that really care about anyone or anything but themselves. Most are on ego trips fueled by their own success and a taste for power. All but a tiny portion of these wunderkind wannabees have done much more to help themselves and their friends than they have to assist the middle class or poor of our nation in any way, shape or form.

It might be a good idea for all the millionaires and gazillionaires running for election this time around to take a couple of hours out of their busy schedules to watch a film that may help them to reconnect with reality and, perhaps, humanity. It's A Wonderful Life is a 1946 Frank Capra movie that stars Jimmy Stewart as George Bailey, a man who didn't know his own worth and value to the community until after he had a chance to see how things would have turned out if he had never been born.

During one of the key moments of the film, George delivers a scathing rebuke to his nemesis Mr. Potter. Potter is a slum lord and exploiter of the poor and middle class in their town who would rather these folks live in one of his broken down buildings than own a home. George says, "Do you know how long it takes a working man to save $5,000? Just remember this, Mr. Potter, that this rabble you're talking about... they do most of the working and paying and living and dying in this community. Well, is it too much to have them work and pay and live and die in a couple of decent rooms and a bath?"

I just wonder how people like Romney, Obama and the others who live off the wealth and political machines fueled by the work and purchases of the average citizen living in the USA might react to George Bailey's little diatribe. Like the Potter character, they would probably ignore it. After all, their families have homes, food and the niceties that make life occasionally worth living. They will not have to worry about their utilities being turned off or watch their kids try and make it through a weekend or summer with little or nothing to eat until the next free school lunch comes along.

Well, I offer my heartiest congratulations to all the politicos running for office this year. Once again you have proven to all of us that you are all about yourselves. And I also tip my hat to the major political parties who keep pushing the same old politician archetypes on us. They are rich, stupid and their parties feel that for one reason or another they are owed a chance to run for President. It's all about winning and power, not about people.

I used to say that performers should be seen and not heard. It always seems that an actor promoting their newest film or a singer plugging their latest album somehow always manages to say or do something dumb during any one of hundreds of publicity interviews. But lately, I have noticed that most of those show biz folks are sounding better and making more sense than the current crop of creepy politicians.

Why can't George Clooney or someone like him run for president? George has had a lot of girl friends (and all are good lookers I might add), but he has always had the good sense to remain single while dating. That's more than can be said for the current crop of cheaters among the potential candidates. George is liked by liberals and does all kinds of charity work.

If your persuasion is more conservative, how about Gary Sinise for president? People love him on CSI and who can forget Lieutenant Dan Taylor, the character he played and brought to life in such a magnificent way for the film Forrest Gump. Sinise has created his own foundation which does much to help and support returning USA Military Veterans and their families.

If George and Gary do not want the job, let's just cut to the chase: It's Lady Gaga for President! With her fashion sense, she could be the new Jackie O. Her sometimes sexually neutral dress or actions would appeal to anyone and everyone. Best of all, she says and does outrageous things and that appears to be one of the major qualifications for a presidential candidate these days.

Chapter Ten: Politics 2012: Attack Ads and Millionaire Politicians

The stupid and lazy politicians that lounge around Washington, D.C., on the taxpayers dime simply never learn. As we approach another national election season the TV, Radio and Internet political attack ads are flowing like bail outs to big banks and corporations. Why? Because most of them cannot run on their own records. They haven't done anything except make things worse for most Americans and do not want anyone to know it.

It's bad enough to have any number of organizations running their own ads for the politicians and parties they support, but it's just torture to have to listen to how bad one idiot thinks another idiot is over and over again. Well, I'm hear to tell you that recent surveys (and my own sore eyes and ears) tell me that attack ads may have jumped the shark or, to put it in the vernacular of those under forty, people are tuning out.

If are politics are local, as Tip O'Neal (former Speaker of the U.S. House of Representatives) once observed, than I have proof that attack ads are not as effective as they used to be. During the last Mayoral Election in my town the incumbent won despite a massive number of attack ads levied against him by his opponent and her supporters. I mean those puppies were mean spirited, down and dirty, and they ran all day and night until everyone was ready to puke.

Most politicians will place their seal of approval on attack ads or just about anything else that will get them elected. In their eyes it's all worth it because if a candidate wins a national election, they will get to go to DC to eat, drink, be merry and ignore the folks at home once they get there. It's the best job in the whole world and, even if they get caught with their hands in the cookie jar, they probably will be given a pass. They might lose a committee chairperson position or something like that, but the chances of them getting kicked out or charged with a crime are almost nill.

Now I know that no one is Washington is listening or even cares, but I have an observation that may be of interest to my fellow Americans and something they might want to consider before they vote in primaries, caucuses or whatever other processes exist to choose their next congressional, senatorial or presidential candidate. It's something I have thought about a lot lately as I have heard from or about people down on their luck.

Don't you think that the person you are planning on voting for should spend as much time and effort on trying to solve the REAL problems that REAL Americans are facing as they do on throwing mud at the other potential candidates and parties or glorying in their own accomplishments? The problem is that those running for office are completely out of touch with the people they want to represent. A good example is the fact that (according to a 2011 poll taken by the Center for Responsive Politics) while only one percent of the people who live in the USA are millionaires, fifty percent of those who serve in congress are worth a million bucks or more.

I am not saying that politicians heavy with cash don't have problems or face tough financial decisions. I mean, trying to figure out what accessories they want to order on their new Escalade or how much hush money they will have to spend to keep a secret lover secret are not easy decisions to make. However, I doubt that most of the folks running for a national political office are going to have to worry about paying their utility bills, their house and car payments, or having enough food on hand for everyone in their family to eat.

I think it's time for some tough love for those who really want to be elected to any national political office. Let's see if they can go two weeks living as millions of Americans are forced to live every day of their lives. Right now I know people that are sleeping in their cars, have no heat on in their dwellings and have barely enough to eat. Let's take potential candidates and make them live under those conditions for a while without their cash, loans from friends or family members, credit cards or anything other than their wits. Let's see if they will be able to access or qualify for all the social problems they claim are out there as a 'parachute' for the poor.

Now I am not just proposing this just as some sort of a joke, I am serious (for once). I want the next candidate or incumbent to experience, first hand, the financial mess they have created and continue to foster. I want them to feel the pain and disgust of people that watch banks and big businesses get baled out to the tune of billions of tax dollars, while the average person cannot even borrow a few bucks from their bank to buy some groceries, get a decent place to stay or put the heat on so that everyone in their dwelling will not get sick from the cold.

I do not expect any politician to learn from an experience like that, because I think that being stupid and self-centered are automatic qualifications for anyone that wants to be elected to national office these days. However, I think it would give a great deal of satisfaction to voters just to know that, for a few days or a even couple of weeks, their next candidate had to spend some time living as millions in the USA are forced to everyday. This also might give any candidate that actually does care a chance to get to know the less than ideal lifestyle of the forty-nine percent of Americans that they complain about who "don't pay taxes."

Chapter Eleven: Is President Mahmoud Ahmadinejad of Iran a U.S. Spy?

Not long ago I was watching 'Homeland' on a cable network. This series is compelling with lots of plot twists and turns. The main premise is that a U.S. Soldier serving in the Middle East is captured, eventually turned and released. He returns home a hero, but that is really just a smokescreen. Terrorists purposely released him to perform the will of his former captors and to be part of a plot to kill American Leaders. The story reminded me of a theory I have had for some time and now am ready to share.

I propose a simple question to you: "Is President Mahmoud Ahmadinejad of Iran a spy or secret operative for the United States? The question seems almost too ridiculous to answer, but before you nominate me for the most idiotic conspiracy theory of the year award, consider some of the facts that I have examined to come up with this outlandish idea.

Ahmadinejad was born in Iran in October of 1956 near Garmsar in the village of Aradan. His father was kind of a jack of all trades and sometimes merchant. His mother was a Seyyede, someone considered to be a direct descendant of the Prophet Muhammad. After they moved to Tehran, Mahmoud's father changed the family's last name which had a negative connotation in city life which linked the family to a not well thought of rural lifestyle. The name Ahmadinejad was chosen because it had a meaning which highlighted the family's kinship to Muhammad.

Today, Mahmoud Ahmadinejad is portrayed by his countrymen as a modest man and devote Muslim with little ambition for self glorification or enrichment. Anyone that has met him will admit that, despite the ever-present propaganda which flows freely from his lips, Ahmadinejad comes across as an intelligent and articulate politician who gives very careful thought to everything he says or does before he says or does it.

In 1976 Mahmoud Ahmadinejad began the process which eventually lead to his enrollment as a student at the Iran University of Science and Technology as an undergraduate student of civil engineering. If we judge intelligence by college entrance exams, it is noteworthy that he scored in the top 200 of over 400,000 Iranians that applied. Ahmadinejad eventually earned a PhD in transportation engineering in 1997 while he was Mayor of a province in Northwest Iran.

It was during what we call the Iranian-American Diplomatic Crisis or Embassy Hostage Crisis which began in November of 1979 that facts about the life and activities of Mahmoud Ahmadinejad become very unclear. File footage and photos from those days when fifty-two Americans were taken hostage by 'Iranian Students' seems to clearly show that Ahmadinejad was one of those 'students.' However, not all the former hostages agree with that conclusion.

It is more than interesting that almost all the higher ranking members of the military that were taken hostage by the Iranians claim that they did not recognize Ahmadinejad as one of their captors. Others including embassy staff and low ranking members of the military are certain that Ahmadinejad was involved. This should still be a huge controversy because it leaves an important matter with great legal consequences unresolved.

My eyes may be deceiving me, but looking at those old films and still photos from the taking of the U.S. Embassy in Iran seems to clearly show a young, but easily recognizable Ahmadinejad leading several of the blindfolded American captors into one of the embassy building doors. Despite the photographic evidence and statements from the majority of the former embassy hostages, the C.I.A. and representatives of the Iranian government say it was not him. Both entities allege that they did their own investigations into the matter and cleared Ahmadinejad.

If Mahmoud Ahmadinejad was, in fact, one of the 'students' that stormed the walls and took hostages at the U.S. Embassy in Iran in 1979, he is a Terrorist that should be arrested the moment he sets foot in the USA for the next meeting of the United Nations. It is silly to believe that he has not been arrested because of diplomatic considerations. If that were true, Saddam Hussein of Iraq and Manuel Noriega of Panama would still be in power. Some other consideration is at work here that the C.I.A. and unnamed members of our government clearly support.

It did not take Ahmadinejad long to become an important part of the new government after the Islamic Revolution in Iran. Unlike others who supported the revolution or took part in the embassy hostage affair only to find themselves eventually dead or disgraced because they butted heads with various influential Muslim clerics, Mahmoud has managed to speak his mind and remain intact. It was almost as if some unseen force (and it probably was not Allah) was protecting him, covering all his tracks and making others believe he was essential to their cause.

Since becoming President of Iran, Ahmadinejad has spoken his mind many times and not always agreed with the most influential of Muslim Clerics in his nation. He has taken these actions without any obvious fear of retribution that can be easily noticed. He has also done some other things that seem a bit strange for a man whom the western powers paint as a maniacal religious and political Ideolog.

While taking a more extreme religious stand on things like men and women using separate elevators in government buildings in Tehran as Mayor of that city, he advocated free and unrestricted travel from province to province (for both men and women) without the need for government issued documents or permissions after he became the nation's president. If people could travel without being tracked by the possession and use of permits, passes or visas, that could certainly benefit those who might want to do so secretly or without being detected.

Mahmoud Ahmadinejad immediately went against the grain of most hard line clerics after being elected President in 2005 by suggesting a list of people to fill cabinet minister posts that were likely to support decisions to keep Iranian Oil flowing to the west regardless of the political or religious consequences. All the names on his list were summarily rejected by the Iranian Islamic

Consultant Assembly (Parliament). He did the same thing after the 2009 election, again suggesting appointments that were rejected.

Ahmadinejad enjoys the public support of Supreme Leader Ali Khamenei who said that he should remain president for at least another five years just before the 2009 national election. Although he does not always agree with the clerics, Mahmoud Ahmadinejad is good at maintaining the bottom line in Iran. Despite sanctions and economic downturns, he has managed to keep the economy on a steady path by reducing inflation and unemployment. However, it is generally agreed that his policies have benefitted the more affluent members of Iranian Society and hurt the poor. Is this on purpose?

Iranians with substantial assets probably have some influence with their government and are unlikely to agree with anything that threatens their wealth. That includes any calls to take the kind of provocative actions that might cause other nations to buy less Iranian Oil or isolate Iran as a rogue nation by passing economic sanctions against it. Although it always seems that Iran is trying to appear to be the bastion of Islamic jihad or extremism, not everyone in that nation wants such a reputation for their country and I believe that Ahmadinejad is one of those who does not despite his rhetoric.

If we carefully examine what Iran is evolving into as an Islamic Nation, we can see that the same two sides are at odds in that nation that have always been involved in a struggle for power. On one side there are those more affluent citizens (or those that want to be) who wish to enjoy their wealth unfettered by the unreasonable mandates of Islamic Clerics. On the other side there are the poor and somewhat economically stable in terms of low paying jobs that feel they have nothing to loose and heaven to gain by following and obeying the clerics.

Under the Iranian political system, the President of Iran does not possess the ability to act at will or make decisions that others will not support. He has to perform a delicate balancing act by saying one thing, doing another and keeping all sides reasonably satisfied. Is it unreasonable to believe that Ahmadinejad is doing just that and more by keeping extremist, devote and moderate elements of his nation feuding in a way that benefits the United States? While doing this, he has been working to greatly reduce poverty and, therefore, reduce the numbers of those who might tend to naturally support extremism or obey the clerics without objection.

Ahmadinejad is clearly interested in building up the middle class of his nation. He has called for the use of a special fund that comes from a portion of oil revenues to help young men get started in life with education, employment opportunities, the ability to purchase a home, business or property, and to be able to afford to get married and start a family. These are the basic elements needed to build a strong middle class that would be unlikely to support actions that might threaten their family or lifestyle.

Despite the appearance that he is not concerned with the rights or advancement of women in Iran due to his Islamic views, Ahmadinejad stated that he expects fifty percent of Iranian Men and Women to enroll in Medicine, Dentistry, Pharmacy and other professional programs at various Universities throughout the nation as soon as they become old enough to do so. To help this along, he recently told a number of older teachers and professors at Iranian Universities that they would eventually have to retire or quit to make room for younger ones that would soon be ready to take their places. Once again we see a program aimed at creating a larger and more stable middle class.

The Ahmadinejad Government is often criticized for being corrupt and showing favoritism to political cronies. Some of Ahmadinejad's appointees have been discovered as frauds with fake university degrees. Why would he risk his position and reputation as a devote Muslim just to appoint people without the proper credentials? He probably would not unless someone told him to do this for reasons as yet unknown or unclear.

Despite his possible involvement with the 1979 embassy hostage crisis, rhetoric and the extreme positions he has taken against Christianity, Judaism and the ways of western civilization, Mahmoud Ahmadinejad seems completely at ease when he visits the USA. He doesn't worry about being arrested, attacked or killed and appears more at ease then the reporters who cover his visits. Why? Considering his comments about Israel, I would think that someone in the Israeli Government would try to assassinate him when he travels abroad to protect the safety and interests of that nation...unless they were asked or told not to!

If we amputate many of the things that people have been lead to believe occur at his behest, Ahmadinejad's actions do not match up with his words. Remember, he is not the only one in charge and there are lots of factions that have access to arms and explosives made in Iran that could be exporting these things for use in terrorist acts. It is sad to believe that if he were a U.S. operative of some kind , all the munitions that flow out of Iran and cause harm to U.S. Soldiers might be considered to be a kind of 'collateral damage' worth the effort of keeping him in place. But let's face it, we have never been a nation that stands fully behind the members of our military or minds watching our best and brightest die just so that a particular foreign policy can be enforced.

Watching 'Homeland' answers the question of how someone that you believe could never be turned might respond to a particular argument, point of view or incident and move away from his or her core beliefs and national allegiances. Because we know so little about Ahmadinejad, it's entirely possible that the U.S. Government was able to exert influence or pressure on him in a manner that we cannot understand for lack of information.

I believe that if you take some time to consider the things I have pointed out, you will discovery that things just do not add up when it comes to our dealings with Iran and Ahmadinejad. From his obvious involvement in the 1979 hostage crisis and high level U.S. government and military denials of the same, to his actions which often run afoul of high level clerics despite his image as a devote Muslim and Islamic purist, none of it makes any sense unless Mahmoud Ahmadinejad is on the U.S, payroll in one way or another.

Chapter Twelve: I Can explain The 'Occupy' Movement

I have to laugh when I watch the various news gathering organizations, political pundits and lifelong politicians try and take on or explain the 'Occupy' crowd. None of these know-it-all's get it. And that's amazing considering that this is the good old USA, a nation born out of public dissatisfaction with its previous government.

The newsies, pundits and politicos keep asking, "Why are they so angry?" and "What is their point?" Well, dummies, let me see if I can explain it to you in a way you'll understand. I will start off by channeling Thomas Jefferson (you know, that guy who wrote the Declaration of Independence). He said, "All tyranny needs to gain a foothold is for people of good conscience to remain silent."

The politicos love silence. They try to keep everyone happy with some food stamps and extended unemployment benefits. When that doesn't work, they try to create jobs that no one ever seems to be able to apply for or even find. Companies get tax breaks and money to hire people, but they don't. Banks get money to lend to people, but they keep it. When that doesn't work they pay for counseling and more medicaid so that doctors can give out pills like candy and keep everyone smoothed out.

Local governments squander or ignore stimulus money: They hire a bunch of new Police Officers or have their current workers fix broken park benches. Instead of hiring more teachers (or helping current educators to keep their jobs), opening a few new trauma centers or helping people pay their electric or heating bills, they split the money up among businesses owned by their favorite 'fat cat' contributors (all in the name of Community Improvement).

Now, here is my take on the whole thing: People are out of work or homeless because their government is more interested in bailing out billion dollar corporations than giving folks a couple of bucks to get by on during a financial crisis that politicians helped to create. Well, a government like that gets what it paid for. Many people have no jobs, no homes and lots of time on their hands. I believe that the 'Occupy' movement is made up of people that decided to send a message to a government intent on not receiving it. Occupying places is the only way they could do send that message and get noticed.

The sad truth is that is understand the 'Occupy' folks, but I also know that they don't have even a glimmer of hope of getting big business or big government to see things their way. Even if they use their vote to express their dissatisfaction, nothing is going to change. Will a congress largely made up of millionaires who consider themselves better than the rest of us care if some kids can't get food stamps because their mom has no way of getting to the food stamp office or if some ninety year old woman who once contributed to this country now has to hope she will not freeze to death this winter because heating assistance is being cut? You know the answer and so do I.

I'm not saying that the government should try and solve everyone's problems, just the ones that they have created. They allowed our economy to spiral out of control by kissing the butts of big banks and corporations. Even after these banks and businesses screwed everyone into the ground and left hundreds of thousands of people destitute and homeless, good old Uncle Sam couldn't wait to line their pockets with lotsa cash.

If the news media, political pundits and politicos think things are bad now when it comes to the growth of the 'Occupy' movement, just wait and see what comes next. Homeless and hungry people get very desperate very fast and none of them are in the mood for election year promises they know will never be kept. That ship has sailed.

People talk about programs to help the poor. How about a problem to help the absolutely desperate and ready to give up? I would say that describes a whole bunch of people in this "world's richest nation" right now. If they want to see change, give every citizen with a low or non-existent income a one-time lump sum of just a few thousand dollars and see how things change.

Don't make it some weirded-out tax break or silly grant that no one can seems to qualify for, make it the real deal. Cash money that, even if it's just a couple of thousand dollars per family, could change lives. People would be able to catch up on their rent, get a cheap car so they can job hunt in a wider area, keep from being thrown out in the street or stay alive another year without having to beg for help from friends, family or community charities. All this would bring new hope, but good luck getting anyone in Washington, D.C. to care enough to even try it.

I'm sure some of you are thinking that another government give-away is a really bad idea. Well, don't worry about it. Politicians are too selfish and self-centered to ever even consider it. They would rather social engineer our nation's way out of poverty by giving money to companies they favor and that, ultimately, will help line their own pockets with campaign cash. There is just nothing in it for them to help their fellow Americans who are down on their luck.

Considering all the occupy movements out there, it might be time for the D.C. crowd to consider the fact that our nation was founded on Revolution. And with all the people that are getting more desperate by the day, we might not be that far from a new Revolution. If anarchy breaks out, you and I can fairly and justly affix the blame at the doors of the White House and Congress. It's time for the newsies, pundits and politicians to GET the 'Occupy' movement before they GET you.

Epilogue

O.K. I have given you a lot to think about...or not...and that's it for now. But I have other books and you can check them all out on Amazon or at my web site: http://gthomy.tripod.com/pp/pp.html (and there is auto re-direction for my mobile friendly clone site as well). Good night and don't let the politicians bite you (where the sun doesn't shine).

See ya...

www.ingramcontent.com/pod-product-compliance
Lightning Source LLC
Chambersburg PA
CBHW070123010626
45794CB00012B/1249